Min  ...motion

Danika Rennie

Mindless Emotion © 2022 Danika Rennie

All rights reserved.

No part of this publication may be reproduced, stored in a retrieval system, or transmitted, in any form or by any means, electronic, mechanical, photocopying, recording or otherwise, without the prior written permission of the presenters.

Danika Rennie asserts the moral right to be identified as author of this work.

Presentation by *BookLeaf Publishing*

Web: www.bookleafpub.com

E-mail: info@bookleafpub.com

ISBN: 9789357619707

First edition 2022

*To all those that stare in the mirror wondering
who they actually are*

ACKNOWLEDGEMENT

Thank you for still being here. For holding on.
Thank you to my mom, my biggest inspiration and my best friend. Who saw the writer in me when even I couldn't.
To my sister, thank you for listening to all my stories, reading all my work, and dealing with all my shit.
To my grade 1 teacher, who thought my writing was so good that she stole it to put on display. It gave me the confidence to start putting my work out there.
To my high school English teacher, who helped me fall back in love with writing. Taught me it was always okay to make mistakes, as long as something was learned or a risk was taken.

Half Empty Glass

I yearn for the days
Where I didn't feel pain
And trauma
Was just a word in a book.

And I look at my glass
My half empty glass
And ask
Why do I feel so fucking sad?

Because the monsters
That haunt me
Are only a dream
In my head.
A nightmare.
Let it be.

Yet it plagued me in the day
Not going away
And my half empty glass
Just makes me feel so empty and sad.

So I empty the glass
And the pain starts to pass
And I'm no longer empty and sad

Because the drink
Made me think
The sadness away
And all I'm left with
Is an empty body
Who can't find her way.

Honey Rose

Her eyes were made
Of sweet honey rose
Pulling you in
For that sick sticky liquid

God.
I'm staring
But I'm stuck
In that sweet honey rose

Those ruby red lips
And teeth blindingly white
And god I'm staring
But I'm stuck
And I don't want to leave
Can't leave
That sweet honey rose

Silence

I've learnt to cry silently
For no one else to hear
I've been hurt
And cracked
And broken
That I've learnt to cry silently
And no one bothers to hear.

I'm Falling

Falling in love
Not a power
But a punishment
Not a gift
But torture

Falling in love
Is a weakness

Falling in love
Is giving your life
To somebody else
And it's all fun and games
Until someone gets hurt

Vulnerable
Weak
Naive
Stupid
Reckless
Hopeless
And so the walls
Go up.

Falling in love
Is not an addiction
I'll ever let myself
Indulge in
Once more.

But then he texts
My cheeks stretch
Sometimes it's funny
Others melancholy
But he texts
And I smile
And the walls
Fall in a pile

Because even though
Love is a curse
Dangerous
Deadly
In the end
I would give my life away
If only to be with you.

Love is vulnerable
But if it lets me
Love you?
Crush me
Hurt me
It'll be worth it.

Your Poet Is Dying

I wish you knew
About the poet you grew
The girl that you broke
Is empty of hope
The girl that you shattered
Thought nothing even mattered
Because the poet you made
Just wants to fade
Away

Blue

Eyes of ocean blue
Take me home
To you.

Pulling me in
Under
Not breathing
Not drowning
Stuck.
Breathe.

Intoxicated
By those liquid eyes
Meeting mine

One step closer
It won't hurt
I love you
Do you
Love me too?

Please love me
Oh beautiful boy
Owner of eyes
Of ocean blue

Physical

Take me
Feel me
Show me
You love me

Physical
Isn't difficult
It shows me
You love me

Touch me
Throw me
Lay your hands
Upon me

Skinny
Body
Why don't
You want me?

Pretty face
Tiny waist
Touch me
Don't you love me?

Why
Don't
YOU
Love
me.

Want
me.

Illusion

Breathe in
Breathe out
5
6
7
8

In perfect
Synchronization

"I love-"

Shhh
Our souls are speaking

Look in my eyes
Nowhere to hide
No disguise

This is real.
You are real.
You.

Fucking beautiful.
I love you.

Reality

Nothing is real
My body
Is not mine
You took it
Ripped it
To indiscernible pieces

Nothing is real
Smiles are fake
Don't
Falter
Don't
Break.

Empty eyes
Colourless skies
My body
Is not mine
A shell
Take the wheel.

Motions.
Routine.
It's not.
Me.

Nothing is real
It
C A N ' T
Be
R
 E
  A
   L.

Mindless

My mind
Is a palace
A sanctuary

Memories
In the basement
Key
Thrown away

Childhood?

My mind
Is a palace
Mine.

A vast expanse
Go for a walk
Lost

Trees of memories
Grown
Matured
Manipulated
Into something
Worthwhile.

My mind is a forest
The palace is forgotten
Dethroned
I get lost

My mind
Is not mine
Too many trees
No clear path

Can't see straight
Can't think straight
Cut them down
Need to think

Cut.
Deeper.
Not enough.
Carve out the roots
Grounded within
Pain.

Cut
Cut
Cut
Trees bleed red.

Don't feel a thing
No thoughts
Pretty red

My mind is a palace
Calm
Loudly quiet
The key?
Thrown away.

Small Box

I don't fit.
In your tiny
Little
Box

Conforming
Compressing
So small
Don't eat
Don't breathe

Help.

Crushed
Collapsed

I can't fit
In your
Tiny
Fucking
Box

I'm sorry.

Stuck

My whole life changed that year.
2012.
The last year of innocence.
Last year of elementary
But for me?
It wasn't the last of anything.
It was the pin that popped my tiny
Protective
Bubble.
The day that hell froze over,
And I got stuck,
Forever.
That innocent little girl
Forgotten.

Passive Suicide

I want to kill myself.
In broad daylight.
Where everyone can see.
This is a cry for help.
Someone come save me.

You see,
At night,
The stars are out
Laid bare.
Beautiful.
A whole endless world
Full of possibility.
It gives me hope.

But then the sun cries awake.
Dreams cease.
Expectations,
Commitments,
Involuntary duties,
Close in.

The day is suffocating.
Night; fleeting.
I can't help but think
I want to kill myself.

Don't

Open door
Shoes off
Toss shirt
Bra falls

S T O P

Jackets forgotten
Drunken stumbles
Down the stairs
Towards the bed

S T O P
N O

Pushed down
Naked
Exposed
Vulnerable

I DO NOT want THIS

Takes
Breaks
Cracks

please stop

Wet tears
Are not pleasure.

Finished.
Broken
Used
Stripped bare
Abused.

Who Are You?

I don't know
Myself.
I wish
I could meet them

Talk for hours
Neverending...
Content in my head.
My voice is theirs.
Their voices are mine.

I dream
We'd be friends

It's just a dream.

Because I don't know
Who they are.
Who
  I
Am.

Void

I feel comfortable
In the dark.

The silence
Welcomes me

The emptiness
Calls me home

I feel comfortable
In the dark.

Lifeless.
Floating.

Free.

Mania

All consuming
Head is racing
Happy?
Sad?
No time to feel
No time to think

No sleep
Don't need
Anything

Floors spotless
Just watch this

Laundry done
New book written
Home work left
End of the week
End of me

It ends.
Overwhelming
Sadness
Engulfed.
Consumed.
Goodbye.

Never Me

I don't think
I'm okay

Playing the part
Of the pretty doll.

My mind is not empty
Is not
Devoid
Of emotion

Except when it is
And I come to you
To feel something
Anything

My brain may not work
But my body does
Routine
Go through the motions
It's not me
Never was
Never will be

So use it
This body
Take what you want
When you want
I'm done.
It's not me.

Printed in the USA
CPSIA information can be obtained
at www.ICGtesting.com
LVHW010826280324
775711LV00002B/314